FAIL-SAFE ELECTRONIC VOTING:
Saving America's Democracy, from an Oligarchy

By

Jim Green

DEDICATED TO:

ABOLITION of the Electoral College—a dinosaur in the Age of Space Travel—where twice in the past 16 years the majority of Americans have cast a resounding vote for the person they wanted to be our president— only to see the office go to someone else......and setting America on a path in distinct contrast to the will of the majority of Americans....

ISBN-10: 1540778487

ISBN-13: 978-1540778482

PROLOGUE

Visualize that Wal-Mart handed us a piece of paper with the words "trust us" as a receipt for our purchases—and you will have a consummate understanding of the reliability of our vote—in our current electronic voting system, in America.

It is of little value in our calling America a "democracy"—if the method for counting our votes is extremely vulnerable—and this election may have even been hacked by the Russians—we know they hacked our emails....

And while conspiracy theorist's eyes glaze over at the prospect that Trump's election may have Putin's fingerprints all over it.....but the prospect just isn't that remote....and in a twist, Trump's pre-election pronouncements that this election has been "rigged" may have been a pre-warning, from "inside information"....just a random thought.

TV personality Chris Hayes on MSNBC ["All In with Chris Hayes"] several years back said that he trusted the results of our electronic voting because the results paralleled the polls—which this election tossed straight into a cocked hat—

AND this is the reason why we all need to get behind Jill Stein in her comprehensive investigation into what actually happened in this election....particularly in the Rust Belt—and while unlikely to change the result--her efforts on behalf of the American people is the highest form of citizenship—a true patriot....

In my book MY LETTERS TO PRESIDENT OBAMA [published on June 10, 2012], and several books since I have included a proposed system to fix our electronic voting, as a chapter, included here:

THE FAIL-SAFE ELECTRONIC VOTING ACT

1) EVERY electronic voting machine (hereafter EVM), must be inexpensive, identical throughout the U.S. in a 1/150 ratio, and *must count and produce a hard-copy of the recorded votes.* In addition, an extra copy of their recorded votes would be produced (not necessarily a hard-copy), marked "Voter's Copy", and containing "NOTICE: Do Not Destroy Until Every Election On Your Ballot Is Certified". [If Wal-Mart handed us a piece of paper with the words "trust us" as a receipt for our purchases—we would be outraged—and yet, this is our current electronic voting nightmare—and in this case it is more than our pocketbook at risk—it is our democracy at risk]!

2) *After confirming that their votes are recorded*

correctly, the voter would then insert the hard-copy ballot into a software-free (count only) optical scanner (hereafter OS), for a second count. The hard-copy ballot would be retained by election officials in the event a candidate asks for a recount (*not possible under the current system, and which undermines the legality of each such election*). The EVM and the OS must be manufactured by different companies (which is universally true today).

3) Election officials assigned to oversee the EVM, would be prevented by law from overseeing the OS, and vice-versa, and stiff criminal penalties would be imposed for violations.

4) Further, every EVM would be programmed with raw data re the total registration rolls, by party, and norms for their voting history, etc.,----as an "alert" to a possible irregularity, such as an "under-vote"—or "vote-flipping" etc., and *standards* established to suspend certification where there is an "improbable result", at least temporarily, of a particular election until the discrepancy is cleared up. (This is what computers do best, and it would be very easy to create such a program).

5) At the end of the election day, tallies would be taken from the EVM and the OS, for each candidate. *If the tallies didn't balance for any given election, or if there is an "alert", that election cannot be certified until the "error" is corrected.* If the candidates agree (the victory is certain), minor discrepancies in the count could be disregarded. While probably rare, the Voter, or a

random sample of Voters, would be required by law to return their Copy of the recorded votes to the election office to clear up any "error", or where an "alert" signals the need for same.

6) Further, every state provides for a recount when the total vote falls below a certain percent of difference between the candidates, impossible to conduct with the current EVM. And thus Congress must mandate the following regarding presidential candidates: A RUN-OFF election is mandated and triggered in those states where the percent of total vote is less than .5% of difference between the two candidates; said election to be held on the second Saturday following the election, on PAPER BALLOTS ONLY, and contain ONLY the names of the relevant candidates, for instance: "Barack Obama, Democrat" and "John McCain, Republican"— with oversight in counting by a representative(s) of each party—said procedure providing more than adequate time to meet the Electoral College mandate [Ideally, all of this could be eliminated if we did away with the Electoral College, but until then….]. NOTE: Had this been the law in 2000, Al Gore would be our president, and America would have been spared the economic, etc., disaster that followed!

7) Finally, absent the above safeguards, and until these safeguards are in place--Congress must mandate that PAPER BALLOTS, ONLY, can be used in our presidential elections. This is not a "partisan" issue, it is a "pro-democracy" issue. Most importantly, this will return the responsibility for our elections, and our vote counting, back into the hands of the individual voter,

where it belongs, and out of the hands of "corporate control"---*it is after all "our democracy", itself, that is at risk if we don't take these steps---and in that regard, is there any time or cost differential that is too great?*

A primary thrust in this book, however, is a corollary issue—Job Creation.....which will never be fixed until the American people get a handle on our electoral process—and we again have a seat at the table in creating "JOBS, JOBS, JOBS"—which has been the mantra in every elecion—with varying degrees of intensity—since the mid-1970's when the world economy unwent a major paradygm shift [more on this throughout].....and in an odd twist—laid the groundwork for a Trump presidency.....

Our economy, today, is what it is....for instance, robots/automation, alone, are resulting in fewer and fewer jobs—the further we advance into the 21st Century—and yet, our job creation model, today, is still lodged in the 18th Century—with our evolving sabotaged because it is propagandized to be "communism, or socialism, or God forbid "liberal"— i.e., our economy is being suffocated by idiocy!

It has given the book "What's The Matter With Kansas?"—a whole new twist.....the premise in "Kansas" asks why on Earth would poor people vote against their own economic interests [why on Earth would they vote Republican?]—

The twist, is that many in the 1%'s want to relegate American employees to A POOL OF SLAVES: To Be

Used And Discarded "at will" [they have spent a fortune since WW II, buying politicians to cement "at will" employment in every state—only Montana limits to probationary employees—and to destroy labor unions in America]—but with "automation", alone, eroding our consumer base—the twist is that clinging to these 18th Century notions eats into corporate profits!

Unemployment is a *No One Wins* –the jobless lose, civility loses [Ferguson, et al], and the Market loses, to wit:

THE LAW OF DIMINISHED INCOME TO THE MARKET FROM UNEMPLOYMENT [hereafter D/UE LAW]

3% is the zero-sum threshold above which unemployment triggers inflation by diminishing labor training and skills, under-utilizing capital resources, reducing the rate of productivity advance, increasing unit labor costs, reducing the general supply of goods and services--and the loss in income to the Market is compounded exponentially with each percentage point of increase in unemployment, above 3%.

In short, the Koch brothers [a metaphor, herein, for the 1%] are shooting themselves in the foot by clinging to these 18th Century notions about abolishing Job

Security—i.e., abolishing "employee rights" in America—

In our 21st Century economy—it cuts into corporate profits—and thus it can now be asked—as asked in "Kansas"—Why are the Koch brothers acting against their own economic interests?

For clarity....I am a capitalist....I support, 100%--build a better widget, sell your company for a million bucks, and retire in south Florida—and it is our current job creation methodology that puts this in jeopardy....

As noted...if you question capitalism, today, you don't become a heretic, per se---but rather a communist.....which is patently absurd....and it is this type of sabotage that prevents our applying solutions that actually work in our 21st Century economy.....

And the most glaring flaw in our current methodology is counting on the market to solve our unemployment problem...with the belief that "the market can provide anybody wanting a job, with a job" which has singularly driven our job creation policy since WW II—When in fact, only *once* since WW II has this resulted in an unemployment rate below 3%--IN 1953—leaving millions jobless in its wake, and turning our inner-cities into war zones, with an epidemic of gun violence!

Unemployment has oft severe social consequences—but currently our policy makers don't have a clue how to solve……because they are beholden to the above fraudulent propaganda/belief that the market can provide everybody with a job!

To briefly illustrate, In the mid-1970's the world economy underwent a major paradigm shift—and while economists disagree over why—all agree with Dr. William F. Mitchell that "High and persistent unemployment has pervaded almost every OECD country since the mid-1970's" [with double digit unemployment common in the Eurozone to this day, and youth unemployment north of 25% in Greece and Spain].

As a result of high unemployment in the 1970's, however, America swung into action--and in 1978 Congress passed, and President Carter signed into law a "legal authorization" to henceforth limit America's unemployment rate to "3%", permanently [15 USC § 3101—i.e., at no time should our unemployment in America exceed 3%, as provided by law].

With a ton of cash, however, the 1% has inexplicably prevented this law from ever being implemented. Full employment is a pro-market solution, and given "automation", alone, this law is *indispensable* to the *effective* functioning of our 21st Century economy.

The purpose of this book is to urge the enforcement of this concept [currently HR 1000, in Committee].

Communism, like liberal are used as derisive words in Republican lexicon to sabotage progress….

change....which prevents urgently needed changes---
Our method for solving problems is sabotaged....

If you speak ill of the problems capitalism is incapable
of solving—you are automatically labeled a communist,
or liberal....

The "social issues" which have so enslaved many who
vote Republican...is based on their vision of the kind of
world they would like to see....like a world without
gays, or women who have sex---people who are not
comfortable in their own skin, and all believe "sex is a
sin"—and since the world is moving in another
direction they are convinced that the world is going to
Hell in a hand basket....[Trump's voters]....

And to change gears slightly, when we have tried
"privatization" to solve our social problems—it has
been a disaster:

For instance, essential programs have been cut—such
as the elimination of text books from the Job Corps
education program—to increase profits, and cronyism
has run rampant—

And in our "for profit" healthcare system, billions of
dollars are siphoned away from the premiums we send
in—and do not go to the healthcare of ANYONE—but
rather is used to pay for lobbyists, to make the CEO's
filthy rich—and spent on propaganda ads to keep it
that way!

Further, it attracts a few who see healthcare as a means to get rich, rather than cure the ill....

A few closing comments in the Prologue—As Oscar Wilde averred "The only truly worthless opinion is an unbiased one"—so bias, agreed—but always in the interest in getting at the larger goal—the truth....

Incidentally, I published my first book on my 78th birthday [I am currently 82—so just hang out for the nuggets when I wander...]—and not that I write that fast, or well—the materials were all there for the better part of the past 30 years, give or take, gathering dust—it was just a matter of pulling them together in some order—also, don't believe any book should be over 60 pages, plus/minus— i.e., can be read in the crapper--two hours, max--lol—but it seems best summed up by a very astute observer [wish I could recall their name to give credit]: Persons who write do so because they have no choice [it is a compulsion, an addiction..]—they become an "author", however, when people start reading what they have written....

Finally, a note to the reader—the papers and letters are not in sequence, and apologize for redundancy [please look for the nuggets...Thx--lol]—also, if you are a "typo-wonk"—are more concerned with sentence structure, etc., than content—you probably won't like my writing—and you will find a wayward capital letter, here and there, and appearing out of place and used for emphasis—or a missing page...Hey, I'm and Indie....I chalk most up to editorial license and tongue-in-cheek, self-effacing humor—so apologies, here—[I seriously support: Take what you do seriously, but never yourself....]....

Just look for content, please....THX

CHAPTER ONE

President-elect Trump:

The number one issue by the electorate in this election was "JOBS, JOBS, JOBS, and both Hillary and Trump promised they would create "millions of jobs", if elected—but the critical question asked of neither by our media, is: "What is your method for creating these jobs"?

It is critical because Americans believe we are "moving in the wrong direction" because our methods of Job Creation since WW II DON'T WORK! [ideology has nothing to do with it—the solution lies in "what is effective?"]…..

Since WW II, our method of Job Creation has been based on a fraud—that "the market can provide anybody wanting a job, with a job"…..when even a cursory review of the data reveals that this method of Job Creation has not resulted in an unemployment rate below 3% since 1953! Leaving millions jobless in its wake, created inner-cities with an epidemic of gun violence, and resulted in the rot in Flint, and the Rust Belt!

Further, in 1980, the Republicans doubled down on this fraud with Supply-Side—"Voodoo Economics"—and pitched it to the American people via the snake oil: Cut taxes for the 1% , they will build factories all across our fair land with the windfall of cash [they promise], jobs will rain down like moonbeams, and everyone will have a job in the factory---Yes folks, it is a fairy tale—and pure BS....

In addition to blowing the extra cash on themselves—rather than creating jobs—this "Voodoo" has resulted in excessive unemployment over 70% of the time since 1980 [twice the % of preceding years]—and when the Democrats failed to fix unemployment with the "legal authorization" in Humphrey-Hawkins--currently HR 1000, in Committee—in 2009 [when we could]—a retaliatory electorate filled the House with lunatics in the 2010 election—and Washington has been in paralysis ever since!

The over-arching point, here, is akin to the maxim: Doing something ineffective, or wrong, over and over, and expecting a different result is [fill in the blank]—our Job Creation since WW II—DOESN'T WORK---THE DATA IS THE PROOF! [and President Trump will fail if he returns to Supply Side, as suggested—given "automation", alone, going forward--our ONLY path to fix unemployment in the 21st Century is Pro-Market, deficit-neutral HR 1000, and/or THE NEIGHBOR-TO-NEIGHBOR JOB CREATION ACT (hereafter NTN) Amazon/Kindle].

Jim Green, Democrat opponent to Lamar Smith, Congress, 2000

CHAPTER TWO

POSTINGS ON FACEBOOK

President-elect Trump has promised "millions of jobs" if elected....his ONLY means to accomplish this in our 21st Century market economy, is via:

THE NEIGHBOR-TO-NEIGHBOR JOB CREATION ACT [hereafter NTN, Amazon/Kindle]:

A Pro-Market, deficit-neutral, federally mandated Social Insurance, owned by our employed, to provide a fund to hire/train our unemployed. For a modest 4% of salary policy cost, triggered by the "legal authorization" in Public Law 15 USC § 3101 [currently HR 1000, in Committee], Trump will create more "private-sector" jobs IN 6 MONTHS, than the failed Republican snake oil to cut taxes for the 1% and pray they will create jobs--rather than spend the windfall of cash on themselves as they did before—IN 6 YEARS!

The Carrier jobs deal is to perpetuate a lie, a fraud on the American people—and the reference is not to the taxpayer's corporate welfare to make it work, but rather the lie that "the market can provide anybody wanting a job, with a job"—the fairy tale job creation policy that has not resulted in an unemployment rate below 3% in America since 1953—has turned our inner-cities into war zones, with an epidemic of gun violence! Further 800 jobs is a joke, when we need to create 200,000 jobs a month in America, just to keep up with our birthrate….in any event, IT IS IMPOSSIBLE TO BE A CHRISTIAN, AND VOTE REPUBLCAN, Amazon/Kindle

For clarity…..Defining oneself as a Christian, is to follow his teachings—BY DEFINITION—why else would anyone call themselves a Christian? And the Republican agenda, today, is a repudiation of EVERYTHING Christ stood for, and spoke out against—thus the book—

CHAPTER THREE

Fareed Zakaria, GPS, et al….

When we start with the mind-set that "We have far more work that needs to be done in America, than we have persons to fill these jobs"—we come out with a far different result in solving our unemployment crisis—and whether the powers that be want to admit it, or not—WE HAVE AN UNEMPLOYMENT CRISIS IN AMERICA [and throughout the OECD]!

It is the reason over 70% of Americans believe "We are moving in the wrong direction!"….

Also, by approaching this crisis with the above mind-set it cultivates the imagination to focus on real solutions…..to think of real work that needs to be done, that is currently ignored……

And at present, we are stuck with the totally fraudulent mind-set that "our unemployed are lazy and don't want to work"…..which has PREVENTED us from finding a solution for OUR UNEMPLOYMENT CRISIS!

Since WW II Americans have been stuck with the BS that "the market can provide anybody wanting a job, with a job"—and this fraud, perpetrated on the American people, has not resulted in a UE rate below 3% since 1953! Leaving millions jobless in the interim—and created an epidemic of gun violence!

The bottom line is that unemployment is a NO ONE WINS—the jobless lose, civility loses [Ferguson, etc.,], and THE MARKET loses, to wit:

OUR SLUGGISH ECONOMY RESULTNG FROM THE LAW OF DIMINISHED INCOME TO THE MARKET FROM UNEMPLOYMENT [hereafter D/UE LAW]

Short Definition:

> 3% is the zero-sum threshold above which unemployment starts substantially undermining the Market--and the loss in income to the Market is compounded exponentially with each percentage point of increase in unemployment, above 3%.

We have several deficit-neutral/Pro-Market paths to Full Employment—and all being sabotaged by BLIND GREED…..for one, HR 1000 [in Committee]—proposed, here, is: THE NEIGHBOR-TO-NEIGHBOR JOB CREATION ACT [hereafter NTN] Amazon—a federally mandated, Social Insurance, owned by our employed to provide a fund to hire/train our unemployed. Jobs beget jobs, and for a modest 4% of salary policy cost will create more "private-sector jobs" in 6 months, than HR 2847, in 6 years!

Specifically, every local jurisdiction in America would be eligible for a Grant-In-Aid from the Labor Department—with this Act triggered by the "legal authorization" in Federal Law 15 USC § 3101—anytime our UE rate rises above 3%.

Jim Green, Democrat opponent to Lamar Smith, Congress, 2000

PS Apologize for CAPS—your software does not permit emphasis

CHAPTER FOUR

President Obama/Council of Economic Advisers:

The Democrats lost the election because they DIDN'T FIX UNEMPLOYMENT! It is the reason over 70% of Americans believe "We are moving in the wrong direction"!

But the reason is not from lack of interest, or dedication, on the part of us Democrats—[or even prevented by an obstructionist Republican Congress]---RATHER, it is because we Democrats drank the Kool Aid that "The market can provide anybody wanting a job, with a job".....and we passed The HIRE Act--HR 2847—in 2009 as our Job Creation law—but it is an "out to lunch" law—because it is a "stop-gap" law waiting for the market to solve the problem [as opposed to "renewal funding"]—

And we Democrats then stood on one foot and then the other waiting on the Market to do something IT IS IMPOSSIBLE FOR THE MARKET TO DO [the issue isn't ideological—it regards something THAT DOESN'T WORK]!

But we Democrats went on BELIEVING in spite of the data that this, our method of Job Creation since WW II--has NOT resulted in a jobless rate below 3% since 1953! Leaving millions jobless in its wake, created our inner-cities with 60% minority unemployment, drug economies, and an epidemic of gun violence!

But wishing hope against hope that something will work--THAT DOESN'T WORK—is not limited to us Democrats—and is akin to those folk in the Rust Belt who believe Trump's promise that he will create "millions of jobs"………..

UNLESS, Trump can wrap his brain around the fact that Hunphrey-Hawkins [currently HR 1000] is a PRO-MARKET solution…and given "automation", alone, is INDISPENSABLE to the EFFECTIVE functioning of our 21st Century market economy! AND, that Trump recognizes that unemployment adversely impacts the "bottom line"—i.e., that people do not buy what we manufacture, when they are jobless [which inexplicably is not cited by Democrats that we need to change the dialogue], to wit:

OUR SLUGGISH ECONOMY RESULTNG FROM THE LAW OF DIMINISHED INCOME TO THE MARKET FROM UNEMPLOYMENT [hereafter D/UE LAW]

Short Definition:

> 3% is the zero-sum threshold above which unemployment starts substantially undermining the Market--and the loss in income to the Market is compounded exponentially with each percentage point of increase in unemployment, above 3%..

The Solution: HR 1000 [in Committee], THE NEIGHBOR-TO-NEIGHBOR JOB CREATION ACT

[NTN]Amazon: a Pro-Market, deficit-neutral federally mandated Social Insurance, owned by our employed—to provide a fund to hire-train our unemployed. Jobs beget jobs, and this will create more "private-sector" jobs in 6 mos, than HR 2847, in six years!

Jim Green, Democrat candidate for Congress, 2000

Thank you for contacting the White House!

CHAPTER FIVE

Hey Mitt Romney....re a Third Party....I'm 82,
but I support the real protest by the American people
in this election—and inexplicably ignored by both of
our major parties....to wit:

According to the FEC, I am a candidate for president
on the Democrat ticket, and specifically urge the
codification of a legal right to work, i.e.: "Work shall
hereafter be the legal right of every citizen, and
Congress shall, except for retirement/disability
programs under federal jurisdiction, make no laws
which will abridge the right of any citizen of legal age,
to work and be a productive citizen."

All of the candidates for president have made
grandiose claims that they will create millions of jobs, if
elected.....and fixing unemployment [hereafter UE] has
been the number one issue in every election in America
since 1975......it is the reason over-flow crowds are
showing up at Trump and Sanders rallies.....to protest
a system that no longer works—with excessive UE 70%
of the time since 1980 [twice that of preceding years]....

THE LYNCH PIN IN FIXING OUR
UNEMPLOYMENT CRISIS, IS FIXING OUR JOB
CREATION—

Our tradition for Job Creation since WW II-- and we
are chary to admit that our tradition has one foot on
the plantation—has been: Cut taxes for the 1%, they
will build factories all across our fair land with the

windfall of cash, and jobs will rain down like moonbeams—i.e., and in combination with the propaganda that "the market can provide anybody wanting a job, with a job".

Problem is—this method of Job Creation is pure BS, a fairytale—and given automation, alone, is unworkable in a 21st Century market economy----and has resulted in a UE rate below 3% only ONCE since WW II—in 1953—leaving millions jobless in its wake—it has created our inner-cities with 60% minority unemployment—particularly among youth—with drug economies, and an epidemic of gun violence…

The bottom line is: UE is a NO ONE WINS….the jobless lose, civility loses [Ferguson, etc.,], and the Market loses….people do not buy what we manufacture when they are jobless--It is not outsourcing that is stealing our jobs in America---it is our failure to adapt in a changing world….

The solution: HR 1000 [in Committee]; FULL EMPLOYMENT IS A PRO-MARKET CONCEPT, and THE CASE FOR WORK BEING A LEGAL RIGHT, Amazon/Kindle

Jim Green, Democrat opponent to Lamar Smith, 2000

PS This is both tongue-in-cheek, and dead serious….

CHAPTER SIX

President Obama/Council of Economic Advisers:

Since WW II our method of Job Creation has been based on the propaganda [lie], that "the market can provide anybody wanting a job, with a job"....

And even our "brightest and best", have fallen prey to this erroneous propaganda—BS----for instance, President Carter lost the 1980 election because he failed to grasp the importance of the "legal authorization"—HE SIGNED INTO LAW [15 USC § 3101]--limiting our UE rate to 3%--Carter would have won hands down had he fixed unemployment! And, Democrats—wearing the same blinders, ushered in a House filled with lunatics in the 2010 election—by failing to employ this legal fix to end UE--leaving Washington in paralysis ever since!

Our failure to fix unemployment is the reason over 70% of Americans believe "We are moving in the wrong direction"!

The bottom line is, UNTIL we change the way we create jobs in America—we can forget the slogan by every politician in the 2016 election: "JOBS, JOBS, JOBS"!

The source of this dangerous path is the conservative response to President Truman's FULL EMPLOYMENT BILL OF 1945—to provide employment for our troops returning from WW

II...and the 1% has spent hundreds of millions, since, buying our elections/politicians--to abolish our labor unions, and to instill "at will" employment in EVERY state—only Montana limits "at will" to probationary employees....

But, by being taken in by this BS—Americans have been made to suffer with a method of Job Creation that has not resulted in an unemployment rate below 3% since 1953! Leaving millions jobless in its wake—and in its ineptness has resulted in our inner-cities becoming war zones, with an epidemic of gun violence!

Also, in the interim—from WW II until today—the world economy has undergone enormous socio-economic change—and precipitated by the colliding forces of automation, globalization, technology, etc., reaching critical mass in the mid-1970's—with subsequent "High and persistent unemployment", since....

Further, and as a result of automation, alone, we have had excessive unemployment 70% of the time since 1980 [twice that of preceding years]....

And yet we cling to the archaic and unworkable Job Creation model, above, at the expense of JOBS, and our modern market economy—WHY?

Ref: HR 1000 [in Committee], FULL EMPLOYMENT IS A PRO-MARKET CONCEPT, Amazon

Jim Green, Democrat opponent to Lamar Smith, Congress, 2000

Thank you for contacting the White House!

CHAPTER SEVEN

Over the past several decades observing…and often finding what we are doing a puzzlement [such as pretending the 800 Carrier jobs is anything other than a political gimmick—when we need to create 200,000 jobs a month just to keep up with our birthrate] but through the BS, I formulated some solutions to our social problems that I assert will actually work—and being a capitalist, have identified as "Neo-Capitalism". To distinguish from other programs, and to identify, coined the name: ECONOMIC INCLUSIVISM, and have a book on Amazon/Kindle. Since 1996, I have had a web page on the internet: www.Inclusivism.org My thinking has evolved over the years, and have zeroed in on Job Creation—I believe our solution to unemployment to be the most important issue facing America going forward in the 21 Century—but posting, here, are my proposed solutions, defined as Economic Inclusivism:

ECONOMIC INCLUSIVISM: A 21st Century Solution

[Social/Prison Reforms]
1) We need to re-classify all crime in the future as violent or non-violent, and discard the archaic terms felony and misdemeanor. The word felony has been implanted in the public's mind to mean "armed and dangerous", and yet over 70% of our prison inmates (all felons) are in prison for non-violent offenses. As a result, the term "felony" is distracting us from addressing the real problem....the violent offender.

2) We need a much greater use of "Shock" Incarceration (A sentencing alternative I authored in the 1960's); a greater use of fines, restitution, and probation (both civil and criminal), in lieu of incarceration, and fines paid directly to victims instead of the state all as part of an expanded menu of sentencing alternatives. [We have 5% of the world's population, and 25% of all prison inmates on earth, in our prisons! If we had the same proportion of inmates to general population as the rest of the civilized world, we would have 400,000 persons incarcerated, not 2,200,000, as we do at present! And yet our PR is that we are the most free country in the world? We daily turn non-violent persons into violent career criminals, with over 99% released back into society, making life in America MORE dangerous, not less! And the grizzly stabbing death, in Illinois, of 8 and 9 year old girls, on Mother's Day, 2005, by a recently released inmate, is a textbook example of this inept approach.....when on earth are we going to accept that to whatever degree....we are also part of the problem? Prison should be a last resort, not first!] We can correct this by mandating that our legislatures return to the pre-1988 (pre the Willie Horton ad) standard: For every $1 budgeted for prisons, $5 MUST be budgeted for the education of our children. This appx ratio was not set by statute, but rather by tradition and common sense. At present, we budget more for prisons than educating our youth, and were not becoming a police state?

3) We need to create Federal Regional Diagnostic and Treatment Centers, for the diagnosis and treatment of the violent offender. We have learned a great deal

about violent behavior in recent years (see www.brainplace.com), and yet we do not have a cohesive or concerted national program or policy in America for dealing with this national epidemic and disgrace. The sheer numbers of homicides by handguns, alone, tells the whole story: Canada 151, Australia 57, Germany 373, Japan 19, England and Wales 54, the United States 11,789! When we add in all deaths by guns, including the fact that 9 children are killed by guns everyday in America, our gun violence escalates to a staggering 28,663! Also, we need to allow for voluntary admissions to these Centers, to prevent juvenile and family violence. It is essential that we seek out "problem-solving", not "punishment" oriented solutions, which actually exacerbate crime.

4) We need to pick-up the lead taken by England, in treating drug addiction as a "medical" rather than a "criminal" problem, so that we can EFFECTIVELY curb drug-related crime, and keep drugs out of the hands of our youth. To demonstrate how specious our thinking has become in this area, alcohol and tobacco kill ten of thousands of persons annually, and yet these drugs are not classified as "dangerous". The tiny handful of persons with "addictive personalities" has totally shaped our drug policies while "addiction", in all of its forms, can only EFFECTIVELY be treated with a medical solution. We have wasted billions on interdiction, and yet, youth drug abuse is actually increasing.

[Economic Reforms]
5) To address our insidious practice of "exclusion",

Congress must enforce a citizen's legal right to work (1), as enacted by Congress in "The Full Employment Act of 1946", and as outlined in the Democratic National Platform position asserting "Opportunity to every American". The right to work and be a productive member of one's society is also a human right. Accordingly, we must ratify the following constitutional amendment: "Work shall hereafter be the legal right of every citizen, and Congress shall, except for retirement/disability programs under federal jurisdiction, make no laws which will abridge the right of any citizen of legal age, to work and be a productive citizen." [Our lapse in enlightenment regarding this urgently needed systemic change -- believed by the ignorant and uninformed to be "communism" -- combined with some really peculiar notions about guns, is the cause for almost all violent crime in America. This is a "practical" rather than a "liberal" solution in our 21st Century economy, a point totally lost on ideologues. This is not a "safety net" (the conservative propaganda buzz term to undermine "social" programs), this is recognizing within each of us a "human right". The distinction is as different as night and day. Further, rather than being a wildly radical idea, a recent Zogby poll found that "86% of Americans think the government should provide a job to anyone who wants one", according to the April 4, 2005 issue of The Nation. Economic Inclusivism, however, does not ask that the government provide a job, but rather recognizes within each citizen the legal right to work and be a prouctive member of the society, as a HUMAN RIGHT. Also, For clarity, I am a capitalist. I support limited interference on the part of government in the free enterprise system, and find the ownership of "business", or a government controlled economy, as currently incorporated in both socialism and communism, to be patently absurd. We will always have government controls so that we have safe food, and medicine, etc., and we rightfully should have, that is separate and apart from the government doing, what a free enterprise business can do better. I would vehemently disagree that our recognition within each citizen a "human right" to work and be a productive citizen to be an interference with the free enterprise system, and it would have more of a psychological impact on the individual, than an economic impact on the economy, as it currently exists. A person wishing to become a doctor, will still become a doctor, or a CEO, or bartender, whatever…..people do what is most compatible with their nature and talents and Economic Inclusuvism would not change that. Indeed, it in some cases it would provide a greater assist in their reaching their goal, than is currently available, and it is much more efficient in utilizing our greatest resource: humans, that our current system. Most importantly, it is the right thing to do].

6) To ensure enforcement/fund this legal right, Congress would create a privately owned, federally mandated, mutual insurance plan, with limited ownership by each person who works, which would provide work/training to any citizen who applies. Work could include: Child care for low income working families, building a high-speed rail system, the urgent need outlined by the NEA for School Modernization, the creation of Federal Regional Diagnostic and

Treatment Centers for the diagnosis and treatment of the violent offender [HINT: convert our excessive new prisons into said Centers], repairing our rotting infrastructure (the list of social benefits is endless). As owners of this plan, each worker would vote on proposed national projects and dividends would be paid annually from unused funds. A projected cost of 8% would be less than the worker currently pays for welfare. [Like Social Security and military retirement moneys, Economic Inclusivism would STRENGTHEN, not weaken the business community....these steps are necessary to preserve, not harm capitalism in a rapidly changing economy...Bill Gates became the richest man in the world because of these monies percolating through the economy....If W (and the wacko Neo-Con ideas) was the president in the 30's, instead of FDR, Bill Gates would be on the street with a "Will work for food" signs.....and further this will prevent our further movement down the erroneous path towards communism or towards the other extreme, fascism (our current movement), both of which require a dictator, and the wholesale loss of our civil liberties, to hold the government in place.]

7) Since this program of "inclusion" would address 95% of our social ills (crime, welfare, drugs, etc., and exacerbated in many cases by inept Band-Aid programs), the federal budget could be greatly reduced and our current Federal Income Tax would be replaced with a National Sales Tax, value-added tax, a national lottery, or some combination of taxes other than our current Federal Income Tax. We currently spend 26 billion annually for the Internal Revenue Service, and

corporations and individuals spend trillions trying to get around the Tax Code, all of which is passed on to us, the consumer, in the higher cost of consumer goods.

7a)A Universal Healtcare System is an essential ingredient of a sane society!

CHAPTER EIGHT

President Obama/Presidential Innovation Fellows/Council of Economic Advisers/First Lady:

Both Democrats and Republicans have proclaimed that this election is about "Jobs, Jobs, Jobs" [a direct quote by Trump]—but the reality is that we are at the same juncture in our social/economic evolution—regarding Job Creation—as when us humans believed that world travel was out of the question, because consensus had it that the world is flat…..

For instance, it is universally believed, today, that "the market can provide anybody wanting a job, with a job"—and even our "brightest and best" appear incapable of thinking of Job Creation, except via this prism….

And Exhibit One is HR 2847—the major legislation to address unemployment [hereafter UE], following the Great Crash in 2008….

Officially tagged as the HIRE Act—it is "stop-gap" [rather than Job Creation] legislation--the same as EVERY like act since 1980—in theory, to bridge us over until the market creates all the jobs we need…..combined with magical thinking and the flat world belief that the market could actually do this—as our economy has limped along on a flat tire…

And, when even a casual look at the data reveals that this scheme is absurd—i.e., the above "belief"--*that has*

SOLELY driven our Job Creation since WW II—has not resulted in a UE rate below 3% since 1953! In a few words, the path we are on DOESN'T WORK—and is more at home on a Santa Claus wish list, than problem solving!

And it has left millions jobless in its wake, and has resulted in our inner-cities becoming war zones, with drug economies, and an epidemic of gun violence!

It appears that the mind automatically defaults to ideology as a means to justify staying on a path—year after year—THAT DOESN'T WORK—with words like "capitalism-good", "communism-bad"—when neither is relevant, and common sense, alone, tells us that the mechanic cannot fix the engine, without the proper tools….

In short, we need look no further than Flint to understand the devastating results of UE—and yet we stood on one foot and then the other in our "wing and a prayer" scheme—as Flint, as well as the rest of the Rust Belt rotted into decay…..

We need to change course—because the path we are on DOESN'T WORK—and the result is unconscionable…..

Re: HR 1000 [in Committee], FULL EMPLOYMENT IS A PRO-MARKET CONCEPT, and THE NEIGHBOR-TO-NEIGHBOR JOB CREATION ACT, Amazon/Kindle

Jim Green, Democrat opponent to Lamar Smith, TX, Congress 2000

CHAPTER NINE

Posted on President-elect Trump's website

A German-national informed regarding a long-perplexing question: Why, on God's earth, did the German people fall prey to a monster like Hitler? To which he instantly replied "Because he put them to work"---and with over 70% of Americans asserting we are "moving in the wrong direction", the importance of Full Employment in America is indisputable! To borrow from "Chitty, Chitty…."—We Democrats had the "legal authorization", on the books in 2009---to reduce our UE to "3%"—permanently--but "we muffed it"—and in 2010, a retaliatory electorate filled the House with lunatics, and left Washington in paralysis ever since! Will the Trump presidency recognize, where we Democrats failed---and given "automation", alone, going forward--that our ONLY PATH to create the "millions of jobs" promised, is via the "legal authorization" in Public Law 15 USC § 3101—and enforced via deficit-neutral, Pro-Market HR 1000 [in Committee], or like solution--THE NEIGHBOR-TO-NEIGHBOR JOB CREATION ACT, Amazon? Trump is not beholden to persons who don't know their arse from a hole in the ground—[like President Obama's Job Creation advisers in 2009, and/or will suggest corrupt and unworkable Supply Side]--and Trump has an excellent opportunity to do the right thing on behalf of the millions who voted for him—AND VOTED FOR CHANGE! Time will tell…….Job Creation can easily get lost in ideology— and incompetence takes over—the solution to Job

Creation is based on "what works, and what doesn't"—and getting lost in ideology is absurd! And evidenced by the fact that what we have been doing since WW II doesn't work in our 21st Century market economy! Indeed, given "automation", alone, Humphrey-Hawkins is INDISPENSABLE to the EFFECTIVE functioning of our 21st Century market economy! Jim Green, Democrat candidate for Congress, TX, 2000

Thank You For Your Support

CHAPTER TEN

President Obama/Council of Economic Advisers:

The most important lesson to be learned from our sluggish recovery is that the world has changed, and to keep pace it is imperative that we change how we create jobs.

Historically, every recession since WW II has been followed by a strong recovery--and every credible economic experts agrees that our inability, today, to create jobs [our high unemployment] has been central in our resulting sluggish recovery—

And the impact on the elderly has been the most evident, and one of the hardest hit….

In 2010, and for the first time since 1975 when the Cost of Living Adjustment [COLA] rate was created by law, to protect our elderly and disabled from pernicious inflation—the COLA in 2010 was "0.0"—

There was a COLA adjustment in EVERY previous year….but it didn't stop there and COLA was again flat-lined at "0.0" in 2011, and again in 2016-—while in the same time frame we had a cumulative 12.7% increase in inflation in the same almost 8 years.

And while we can all celebrate the turnaround after the Republicans trashed our economy in 2008--it is evident by COLA, alone, that we have been in an extremely anemic recovery—

The bottom line, however, is the correlation between: "High Unemployment & Sluggish Recovery/Economy" —the former causing the latter.

Since WW II, and the [FULL] EMPLOYMENT ACT OF 1946 [to create jobs for our returning troops], we have had two distinct paths to Job Creation in America:

1] The belief/propaganda [lie] that the market can create all the jobs we need, and....

2] Outlined in pro-market, deficit-neutral Humphrey-Hawkins [hereafter HH] in 1978—that would trigger Job Creation from a "reservoir of public employees" anytime our UE rate rises above "3%".....[currently HR 1000, in Committee].

The plutocracy/oligarchy hated [didn't understand] HH, however, and with hundreds of millions to buy our elections Washington pretty much hated HH too.....i.e., its "legal authorization" has never been enforced....

And evident by our current recovery—with President Obama ill-advised by his Council of Economic Advisers—i.e., given "automation" alone, eliminating jobs it is evident we are long over-due in changing course—we are long over-due in enforcing the "legal authorization" in HH.

Ref: FULL EMPLOYMNET IS A PRO-MARKET CONCEPT, Amazon/Kindle

Jim Green, Democrat opponent to Lamar Smith, Congress, 2000

CHAPTER ELEVEN

The following is a letter from U.S. Representative John Conyers, posted on the internet, re his law--H.R. 1000, the "Humphrey-Hawkins Full Employment and Training Act"

"Since 2000 more than 50,000 manufacturing facilities in the U.S. have closed and roughly 50,000 industrial jobs have been lost each month. Now service sector jobs, where the remaining two-thirds of all workers are currently employed, are disappearing. Because of, but not limited to technology advances, these middle-income jobs are not likely to come back, effectively hollowing out the America's middle class and leaving millions of unemployed and underemployed workers with limited future prospects. The effect of these trends on American jobs were significantly aggravated by the "Great Recession."

"Meanwhile, in spite of the Great Recession, the wealthiest 1% of Americans has become even richer. The share of income taken by the top 1% has more than doubled by 2007, U.S. corporations became flush with record profits, and the stock market has rebounded to all-time highs. All while stagnate wages for the working poor and middle-class remained and, in some cases declined, over the same time period.

"During the Great Depression, President Roosevelt's New Deal put millions of Americans back to work building roads, dams, bridges, parks and electrification systems.

"There is no reason why America cannot have a 21st century "New Deal," where unemployed Americans can be gainfully employed rebuilding our crumbling infrastructure and strengthening our communities. It is my hope that with the reintroduction of my bill, the "Humphrey-Hawkins Full Employment and Training Act," Congress will begin to seriously examine the idea that the federal government can, and must, play a major role in putting Americans back to work. H.R. 1000 is deficit neutral, because it is paid for by a modest tax on stock and bond transactions by Wall Street trading firms. Having already received a significant bailout by American taxpayers, it is only fair that Wall Street pay Main Street back by helping put America back to work."

Sincerely,
John Conyers, Jr.

CHAPTER TWELVE

Letter to the editor:

Will politics never change?

A Republican candidate for president said "On next January 20, there will begin in Washington, the biggest unraveling, unsnarling, untangling operation in our nation's history."

But before Republican ideologues say "right on" regarding their belief in unraveling President Obama's administration— this was from a speech by Republican candidate Tom Dewey, and directed at President Truman, in 1948!

Given the political rhetoric you would think President Truman [and President Obama] couldn't even tie their own shoes— albeit, President Truman had ended WWII [while President Obama has rescued America from another Great Depression, and got bin Laden, etc., etc.,].

And other parallels between these two elections are even more striking. For instance, Truman was outraged by what he called a "Do nothing Congress"— and he went on to warn the electorate that "The country cannot afford another Republican Congress." No informed American will dispute that, today....

The most startling parallel, however, is when Truman said of the Republican Congress on a stump speech "It is a sad tale of the sell out of the American people to these gluttons of privilege— these cold men who skim the cream from our natural resources to satisfy their own greed."

This could have been said yesterday, and yet, it was said by President Truman 68 years ago!

Finally, President Truman offered some words of wisdom to the American electorate on the danger of returning our government back to the Republicans [as true today, as then] "I'm just waking you up to the fact that this is YOUR fight— and YOU are going to be the loser [if you return the White House back to the Republicans]."

And, as every student of History knows, and in spite of the inexcusable headline error by the Chicago Tribune "DEWEY DEFEATS TRUMAN"— President Truman did win—and kept the White House where it belongs— with a Democrat!

Ref: IT IS IMPOSSIBLE TO BE A CHRISTIAN, AND VOTE REPUBLICAN, Amazon/Kindle

Jim Green, Democrat opponent to Lamar Smith, Congress, 2000

Bio: http://www.amazon.com/James-L.-Jim-Green/e/B001KHZIMM/ref=ntt_dp_epwbk_0

CHAPTER THIRTEEN

President Obama/Council of Economic Advisers:

THE OUTRAGE BY BERNIE/DONALD FOLLOWERS?

While we celebrate 255,000 jobs, and a steady 4.9%--in the 8/5/16 Jobs Report—the fact is---the oligarchy/folks running the show in America JUST-DON'T-GET-IT......

We could attribute to "Old habits are hard to break".....and while this cannot be cited as the sole reason—it is a factor---in the oligarchy/Washington's inability to bring our Job Creation in America into the 21st Century....particularly given "automation", alone....

What they "don't get" is that Since WW II our Job Creation in America has been driven by a single premise [propaganda/lie]: "The market can provide anybody wanting a job, with a job"—problem is, it is PURE BS!

And evident by the fact that this Job Creation model has not resulted in an unemployment [hereafter UE] rate below 3% since 1953—and in the interim has created our inner-cities--with 60% minority UE, drug economies, and an epidemic of gun violence!

And there is something quite disturbing when Washington stood on one foot and then the other, and via magical thinking, let Flint, and the rest of the Rust Belt rot into decay—the "magical thinking" was the belief that "No problem"--the market will fix this—particularly when it was OBVIOUS BY THE RESULT, that the market is INCAPABLE of fixing this problem!

An indifference, incidentally, that was infinitely magnified by the fact that since 1978--Washington has had the "legal authorization" to restrict our UE rate in America to "3%"—PERMANENTLY-- [Pro-Market 15 USC § 3101—and currently HR 1000—in Committee]—laws that are INDISPENSABLE to the EFFECTIVE functioning of our 21st Century MARKET ECONOMY!

Unemployment is a NO ONE WINS proposition…..the jobless lose, civility loses [Ferguson, etc.,], and the market loses, to wit:

THE LAW OF DIMINISHED INCOME TO THE MARKET FROM UNEMPLOYMENT [hereafter D/UE LAW]

Short Definition:

> 3% is the zero-sum threshold above which unemployment starts substantially undermining the Market--and the loss in income to the Market is compounded exponentially with each percentage point of increase in unemployment, above 3%.

Ref: **FULL EMPLOYMENT IS A PRO-MARKET CONCEPT; FIX UNEMPLOYMENT, AND THIS WILL FIX THE MARKET; and THE NEIGHBOR-TO-NEIGHBOR JOB CREATION ACT,** Amazon/Kindle

Jim Green, Democrat opponent to Lamar Smith, 2000

PS: Apologize for CAPS—your software does not provide emphasis

Thank you for contacting the White House!

CHAPTER FOURTEEN

President Obama/Council of Economic Advisers:

Two-thirds of the world's 7 billion population live in market-driven economies—1.2 billion are in the OECD, with China and India, alone, adding an additional 2.6 billion, and anyone who doesn't think China is a market economy, hasn't shopped at Wal-Mart....

The over-arching point, here, is the unwritten, but nevertheless pervasive/pernicious belief in our market-driven economies is that "the market can provide anybody wanting a job, with a job"....it is pernicious because it causes the "rank and file" to oppose climate change—in their belief that this is their *ONLY* means to get a Job! And, when, in fact, it is *BS, NOT* supported by the data or empirical evidence....

With the result that our record in job creation is deplorable—i.e., this methodology is woefully inadequate, as we inch along, and 5 years after the declared end of the Great Recession—we still have almost 10 million jobless Americans....

The question *NOT* being asked in Washington is: How do we address our pernicious unemployment in America—when the market cannot create enough jobs?

Had we put a lawnmower engine in the Saturn V rocket, on our Apollo 11 trip to the moon—we would never have gotten there...a perfect metaphor for our current method of job creation in America—which leaves millions jobless for years—and skewed against minorities.....

The fact is, *ONLY ONCE* in the past 65 years—under our "market only job creation" model—has our unemployment rate dropped below "3%"—in 1953—and in spite of the "legal authorization" in the U.S., since 1978, to limit our unemployment to 3% [15 USC § 3101].

In short, at *NO* time since 1978, and to this day, should our unemployment rate in America exceed 3% [HR 1000]---when, in fact, our jobless rate, today, is double that—and it will be 2017 before we return to even an anemic 5.5%, as projected by the CBO--

And the irony is that unemployment is a "NO ONE WINS" proposition—both the jobless lose, and the market loses, to wit:

> 3% is the zero-sum threshold above which unemployment starts substantially undermining the Market--and the loss in income to the Market is compounded exponentially with each percentage point of increase in unemployment, above 3%.

FULL EMPLOYMENT IS A PRO-MARKET CONCEPT [Amazon]

Jim Green, Democrat opponent to Lamar Smith, Congress, 2000

CHAPTER FIFTEEN

President Obama/Council of Economic Advisers:

A German-national advised—in response to a question perplexing me for years—"Why on earth did the German people, with their rich cultural history, fall under the spell of a monster like Hitler"? And without a moments hesitation he said "Because he put them to work".

There is a message in there of vital importance: The value humans place on being a productive member of society—the value we place on "work"—even raising the question if it should become a Human Right?

And while giving lip service to the plight of the unemployed--our market economies, the OECD, which includes the U.S., all suffer from high unemployment— and none address unemployment as a "social" problem—with serious social consequences--WE, as a society have the RESPONSIBILITY to address— Rather they leave the creation of employment up to the whims of the market--And if the market fails, the unemployed are out of luck!

Which raises the question: The market suffers when people are unemployed—and the unemployed suffer when they are not working—so WHY on earth do our market-driven economies continue down such an unrewarding--a lose-lose path—where the market loses, and the unemployed lose?

The late Peter Drucker advocated for CEO salaries being limited to 20 times that of the lowest paid employee [the Swiss recently had on the ballot 12 times]—but it is argued that a brain-drain would occur if we didn't leave this to the market to set CEO salaries—

And whether or not this is true—WHY on earth do we persist in the anachronistic BELIEF that the market can provide anybody wanting a job, with a job [untrue since the mid-1970's]--particularly, and given automation, alone--an expanding and contracting public workforce is an INDISPENSABLE component to the EFFECTIVE functioning of a modern market economy?

Indeed, in the U.S. we have the "legal authority" on the books [15 USC § 3101], to limit our unemployment to 3%--in short, at no time should our unemployment exceed 3%--So why does Washington avoid this legal authority as if it were the plague—such as indifference to deficit—neutral solutions, i.e., HR 870, or via Social Insurance in The Neighbor-To-Neighbor Job Creation Act?

Please see: WHY WE CAN'T FIX UNEMPLOYMENT, Amazon

Highest regards,

Jim Green, Democrat opponent to Lamar Smith, Congress, 2000

CHAPTER SIXTEEN

President Obama/Council of Economic Advisers:

Capitalism is ideal in producing and selling corn flakes and cars—It doesn't work in solving "social problems" such as unemployment and our healthcare....

And when we have tried "privatization" to solve our social problems—it has been a disaster:

Essential programs have been cut—such as the elimination of text books from the Job Corps education program—to increase profits, and cronyism has run rampant—

And in our "for profit" healthcare system, billions of dollars are siphoned away from the premiums we send in—and do not go to the healthcare of ANYONE—but rather is used to pay for lobbyists, to make the CEO's filthy rich—and spent on propaganda ads to keep it that way!

Further, it attracts a few who see healthcare as a means to get rich, rather than cure the ill....

The truth is, we currently have a blended system—and they are, in fact, indispensable to each other:

Were it not for Social Security Insurance moneys percolating up through our economy in 2008—we would not be talking about having narrowly averted another Great Depression—We would be buried in one!

Social Insurance is a vital ingredient in building a vibrant and decent society—And, invent a better widget, sell the company for a million bucks, and retire in South Florida [capitalism]—is as well a vital ingredient in building a vibrant and decent society.

So why do we have this war of words pitting the two against each other—rather than educating the American people regarding the indispensable symbiotic relationship they have to each other?

Were it not for the $2 trillion + Washington infuses into the economy annually—capitalism would fold in a NY Second!

And yet, most Republicans ask God in their prayers at night to be protected from becoming communists, or socialists, or even worse "liberals"—i.e., ignorant of what the terms mean…..

And this war of words disguises that the Republican Party, today, is not the Pro-Market party they boast—

but rather their policies are, in fact, Anti-Market—destructive to capitalism!

Pandering to the GREED of their wealthiest contributors—the Republican One and Only program—is NOT a Pro-Market concept!

Another misnomer in the war of words, is right-wing invented "entitlement"—a word that should be banned from honest discussion—do we refer to our auto insurance as an "entitlement"?

And when Social Security Insurance brings in more that it pays out, i.e., is deficit-neutral--how is that an "entitlement", and why is it portrayed in our graphs as a "government expense"—or even included in these graphs? If a corporation reported a massive loss on a product they in fact made money—they would be charged with fraud in a New York Minute!

The list goes on—please see: OUR GREED AND IGNORANCE, on Amazon/Kindle

Jim Green, Democrat congressional opponent to Lamar Smith, 2000

CHAPTER SEVENTEEN

President Obama/Council of Economic Advisers:

THE HISTORY OF HUMPHREY-HAWKINS

The historic March On Washington, and Dr. King's "I had a dream" speech, in 1963, was a march for JOBS.

At that time, and to this day, our job creation in America has been based on the premise that "the market can provide anybody wanting a job, with a job—

And yet, only ONCE since WW II has this method of job creation resulted in an unemployment rate below 3%--in 1953—leaving millions jobless in its wake.

Following Dr. Kings death in 1968, civil rights leaders, including Jesse Jackson, annually marched on Dr. King's birthday for legislation that would address our pervasive unemployment in America.

Their demand was not without legal foundation. In 1946, President Truman signed into law the [FULL] EMPLOYMENT ACT OF 1946, to provide employment for our troops returning from WW II.

The 1%, however, balked at American employees having rights—particularly a right to employment [the model which exists to this day]—and the law was never implemented.

Ironically, Australia enacted a law similar to President Truman's Employment Act—and for the same reason—and for the next 30 years [and until the ill-winds of neo-liberalism in the mid-1970's] Australia's employment model was based on the premise that "anybody wanting to work should be able to find a job"—with 2% or less unemployment common. Australians still refer to this as their "Golden Age".

As a result of the demand by civil rights leaders for legislation, however, in 1978 President Carter signed into law—what is commonly known as the Humphrey-Hawkins Full Employment Act [15 USC § 3101].

The law provides the "legal authorization" for the creation of a "reservoir of public employees" anytime our unemployment in America exceeds "3%". That is, and to this day—at no time should our unemployment rate in America exceed 3%.

The money in politics, however, has prevented this law from being implemented!

Notwithstanding, a lone Congressman, Conyers [and a growing number of co-sponsors] has diligently worked to implement Humphrey-Hawkins [currently, deficit-neutral HR 1000, in Committee].

And, singularly, unemployment is the most pernicious problem facing America, today….

Ref: FULL EMPLOYMENT IS A PRO-MARKET CONCEPT, Amazon

Jim Green, Democrat opponent to Lamar Smith, 2000

Thank You!

Thank you for contacting the White House.

CHAPTER EIGHTEEN

President Obama:

It is impossible to reform our broken criminal justice system—absent our creating a viable job creation program in America.

And while it is generally believed that we do have a job creation program, in fact, we do not!

We have the BELIEF that "the market can provide anybody wanting a job, with a job"—but the data shows that only ONCE since WW II has this belief resulted in an unemployment rate below 3%--in 1953—leaving millions jobless in its wake-- and has resulted in:

60% minority unemployment in our inner-cities, with drug economies, and an epidemic of homicides [i.e., not fixing unemployment has turned our inner-cities into war zones, and created a breeding ground for our inexplicable incarceration rate].

Further this "belief" has been a stumbling block in finding a solution for our pervasive unemployment--In short, we have not been looking for a solution—because our policy makers believe we have one—and apparently few have looked at the data....

Also, ignored in the discussion is that unemployment is a "social" problem, with adverse, and oft severe social consequences—both for the individual, as well as the larger society [i.e., it is the responsibility of the larger society to solve]—

With tentacles integral to all of the social problems facing Americans, today—for instance, ending unemployment is integral to Criminal Justice Reform, and the repair of our crumbling infrastructure….

Further, in 1975 we spent $5 educating our youth, for every $1 we spent on prisons…..by the mid-1990's [with the American people having been terrorized by the Willie Horton ad—and on an hysterical prison building spree] our competing tax dollars tipped in favor of prisons—and at present we spend more on prisons, than on educating our youth.

The irony in all of this is that we have the "legal authorization", on the books to reduce our unemployment rate to 3%, tomorrow [15 USC § 3101—and deficit-neutral HR 1000, currently in Committee]—and also ignored in this context, is that President Obama had a weapon in addressing our economic meltdown in 2008, not available to FDR—and that is the $800 billion in Social Security Insurance claims percolating up through our economy—and in the absence of which--We would be buried in another Great Depression!

Turning the page—and given "automation", alone, is critical going forward in the 21st Century—and is a "win-win"—the American people win, and the market wins….

Ref: FULL EMPLOYMENT IS A PRO-MARKET CONCEPT, Amazon

Jim Green, Democrat opponent to Lamar Smith, 2000

CHAPTER NINETEEN

I didn't write the following. It is a cut and paste from FACEBOOK, or some blog [would like to give credit if knew the author]--but it is so on target regarding how "fear" is driving Conservative policy in America today—i.e., is undermining America and our progress—and relegating America to a Third World country status, rather than a world leader—FDR had it on the nose in "All we have to fear, is fear itself"…at his inaugural in 1933….

"Conservatives are such cowards: they are afraid of gay people getting married or serving in the military; they are afraid of bringing terrorists to super max prisons in the US from which no one has ever escaped; they are afraid of the boy scouts letting gay kids in; they are afraid of everyone voting and are constantly suppressing the vote under some bogus voter fraud theory; they are afraid of letting students vote at their universities; they are afraid of women having the right to choose; they even are afraid of women getting contraception [the real issue actually is a women's agency and control over their bodies]; they are afraid of immigration reform leading to citizenship because they are afraid of-- name whatever reason; they are afraid of mandating gun purchasers to undergo background checks for crazy people and terrorists; they are afraid of people smoking pot; they are afraid of climate change being real and contradicting their beloved Bible; they are afraid of legitimate campaign reform; they are afraid of Muslims; they are afraid of blacks; they are afraid of atheists; they are afraid of hippies; they are afraid of socialists; they are probably still afraid of monsters under their beds; they are just rank cowards and keep making things up to be afraid of."

CHAPTER TWENTY

[I couldn't resist including this...and yes I am the author.....]

A MESSAGE FROM GOD

MANY CENTURIES AGO, a man of the cloth, we don't know his name, and in a flash of insight (perhaps induced by peyote) told his flock that "sex is a sin". And lo and behold he learned that by taking a very natural and healthy part of our life and turning it into something that was "dirty and nasty", that he could imprison his flock, and fill his coffers, and hallelujah it was a great day for the Lord!

Quickly, his miracle spread to other churches in his village, and then to the next village, and then the next county, and then state, and soon it spread to all the churches in the ancient world, and all of their flocks cowed in fear and shame and became imprisoned, and their coffers over-floweth. Hallelujah, it was a great day for the Lord!

And to keep the myth alive they started inventing stories, half-baked stories, that made no sense to anyone who is rational, such as "Mary was a virgin"—well, she just had to be a virgin because she would never partake in anything that was dirty and nasty, like sex (if you're doing it right), and this was necessary to make "sex is a sin" make sense...so they invented a Mary that was "sinless"--you get the picture. And their coffers over-floweth. Hallelujah, it was a great day for the Lord!

No one seemed to be bothered that when we play tricks on the human mind by taking something that is very natural and healthy, such as sex, and make it dirty and nasty that all kinds of bad things happen to the human mind:

Such as most pedophiles, and most serial killers, and voting Republican, and unwarranted suicides, and most mental illness, and unwanted pregnancies. (Teens not wanting to have sex is the perversion, not the other way around, and by replacing sex education and condoms, with unrealistic "abstinence", and by using blather about "low self-esteem" to shame them into not "sinning"—We have a teen pregnancy in the U.S. twice that of England and Canada!).

But none of this mattered, because their coffers over-floweth, and Hallelujah, it is a great day for the Lord!

There is a cure--------Tell our right-wing hypocrites, who Judge, rather than "Judge not".... to shove it....

GOD

ABOUT THE AUTHOR: I was employed in our Criminal Justice System for a cumulative 20 years as a probation officer, with 5 of those years as a chief probation officer. I authored the concept of "Shock Incarceration" which became law in Kansas in 1970, and then was adopted in numerous jurisdictions in the U.S. and also spread to Europe—it is currently identified in the U.S. as "Boot Camp" [as the means to "shock" the young offender—and a total distortion of my original intent—like many ideas, once released, they take on a life of their own]. I also instigated establishment of the first Court Psychiatric Clinic in the U.S., in conjunction with psychiatrists from the Menninger Foundation, as a chief probation officer. Finally, I was the Democrat candidate for Congress, District 21, TX, 2000. I would most define myself as a Social Ecologist-- [albeit my degree is in Psychology]. My web page is www.Inclusivism.org —which has been on the internet since 1996.
http://www.amazon.com/James-L.-Jim-Green/e/B001KHZIMM/ref=ntt_dp_epwbk_0

\

A BRIEF ADDENDUM: When the U.S. Supreme Court denied certiorari—where the violation of my constitutional rights were obvious, and criminal negligence on the part of the government defendants in the death of our son, equally obvious—[detailed in THE HARVARD BOYS CLUB, Amazon/Kindle]--I filed a Petition for Rehearing [which is automatic]—and included the following. The Clerk of the U.S. Supreme Court called me at my work in California, and asked that I withdraw the "cartoon" [a reprint from The NEW YORKER] from my Petition. I refused on the basis of the First Amendment, and it remains in the archives at the U.S. Supreme Court [Docket #: 79-1627], to this day. The wording [not that clear] is: "Excellent, excellent. A fine blend of truths, half-truths, and blatant falsehoods".

IN THE

Supreme Court of the United States

October Term, 1979

No. 79-1627

JAMES L. GREEN,

Petitioner,

VS.

"Excellent, excellent. A fine blend of truths, half-truths, and blatant falsehoods."

PARTIAL LIST: BOOKS BY THIS AUTHOR ON AMAZON/KINDLE/BN:

- **THE HARVARD BOYS CLUB:** Hitler's Assault On Our Freedoms From His Grave

- **MY LETTERS TO PRESIDENT OBAMA:** Confessions Of A Compulsive Letter Writer

- **OUR GREED AND IGNORANCE:** Poses A Far Greater Threat To America, Than Terrorism

- **LETTERS ON STEROIDS:** Confessions Of A Compulsive Letter-To-The-Editor Writer

- **THE FIRST TIME I HAD SEX:** And, The Religious Intolerance Attack On America

- **WHY PRESIDENT OBAMA LOST THE 2012 ELECTION:** A Wake-Up Call

- **ECONOMIC INCLUSIVISM:** Neo-Capitalism/An Anthology: Inclusive pro-market solutions to our social problems

- **AMERICA IS ONE SICK MF:** Why Greed-Driven America Went Off The Rails….

- **EVERY GIVEN SUNDAY:** A Scientific Formula To Predict NFL Games

And others….http://www.amazon.com/James-L.-Jim-Green/e/B001KHZIMM/ref=ntt_dp_epwbk_0